GW01466092

My First Acrostic

Leicestershire

Edited by Lisa Adlam & Donna Samworth

First published in Great Britain in 2009 by:

Young Writers
Remus House
Coltsfoot Drive
Peterborough
PE2 9JX
Telephone: 01733 890066
Website: www.youngwriters.co.uk

Foreword

The 'My First Acrostic' collection was developed by Young Writers specifically for Key Stage 1 children. The poetic form is simple, fun and gives the young poet a guideline to shape their ideas, yet at the same time leaves room for their imagination and creativity to begin to blossom.

Due to the young age of the entrants we have enjoyed rewarding their effort by including as many of the poems as possible. Our hope is that seeing their work in print will encourage the children to grow and develop their writing skills to become our poets of tomorrow.

Young Writers has been publishing children's poetry for over 19 years. Our aim is to nurture creativity in our children and young adults, to give them an interest in poetry and an outlet to express themselves. This latest collection will act as a milestone for the young poets and one that will be enjoyable to revisit again and again.

Contents

The Poems

Jessica's Poem

J ogging with my pet

E very morning

S ometimes it is cold

S ometimes it is sunny

I like being outside

C an I keep her forever

A nd ever?

Jessica Humphreys (7)
Arley House PNEU School

Amalie's Poem

A malie sees the future through the window

M eaning more trees than there was in the future

A way in the future

L ights pass by in the future

I have looked forward to it, now it's finally here.

E very day is the same.

Amalie Macnaughtan (7)
Arley House PNEU School

Timothy's Poem

T oday I'm really sad

I n Arley House School, it's closing

M oney is important

O h I'm really sad

T imes are going by

H ow can I stop the school from closing?

Y ou can't stop it.

Timothy Macnaughtan (7)
Arley House PNEU School

My First Acrostic

A little alien is crazy

L ittle aliens eat stars

I like aliens

E normous aliens eat children

N aughty aliens do bad things

S limy aliens, yuck!

Lily-Babe Smith (5)
Ashby CE Primary School

My First Acrostic

S pace is far away.

P luto planet is far away.

A liens are funny.

C old planets are silly.

E llen, the alien, is helpful.

R uby planet is sporty.

O ctopuses are in space.

C arry a moon rock.

K ey planets.

E lephants in space do exist.

T homas' planet is good.

Madeleine Boddice (6)
Ashby CE Primary School

My First Acrostic

A liens are nice.

L et's go to meet an alien, would you like to meet an alien?

I like aliens.

E very alien is nice

N o listen, aliens live in space.

Riley Weston (5)
Ashby CE Primary School

My First Acrostic

A liens like eating plants.

L ittle aliens are grumpy.

I love space golf.

E very alien is different.

N o aliens live on Earth.

Jake Hayward (5)
Ashby CE Primary School

My First Acrostic

A liens don't have a nanny.

L ittle aliens are kind.

I like aliens.

E very alien has a mum.

N o aliens live on Earth.

William Jones (5)
Ashby CE Primary School

My First Acrostic

A liens are silly.

L ook at the aliens.

I like aliens.

E very alien is hungry.

N o alien has a brain.

Alfie Reynolds (5)
Ashby CE Primary School

My First Acrostic

A liens' tummies are coins.

L ittle aliens are kind.

I saw some aliens.

E very alien is funny.

N o home life with aliens.

Bethan Haines (5)
Ashby CE Primary School

My First Acrostic

S pace is funny because it has no sun.

P eas in space are dry.

A liens are different and sometimes they're not.

C ome down to Earth with me.

E very alien go home now.

Rebecca Tomlinson (5)
Ashby CE Primary School

My First Acrostic

A liens live on planets.

L ittle aliens have fun.

I love aliens.

E very alien is funny.

N o aliens are cold.

Jonathan Auton (5)
Ashby CE Primary School

My First Acrostic

S pace sometimes is extremely busy.

P arents mostly plant stuff but it takes long.

A liens live on every planet.

C opycat planet is very weird, every time I say something everyone says it too.

E very alien has a child.

R on, the alien, is very greedy, so is her mum and dad.

O n planet Pluto there are loads of aliens.

C ats love aliens so much.

K eys are everywhere in Key World.

E very alien eats lots of food.

T homas, the alien, is very strong.

Noah Rotstein (5)
Ashby CE Primary School

13

My First Acrostic

S pace aliens are sometimes invisible.

P arent aliens are enormous.

A liens don't go to school.

C ute aliens help people.

E ven parent aliens get excited when it's Christmas.

R eal people go to space in a rocket.

O ctopus aliens have eight arms.

C rew aliens can fly.

K ind and clever aliens still talk funny.

E ven ugly aliens speak funny.

T ired aliens can't go to bed because they've got no gravity.

Joe Jenkin (6)
Ashby CE Primary School

My First Acrostic

A liens are grumpy.

I love aliens.

I love little aliens.

E normous aliens.

N aughty aliens do bad things.

S ome aliens are fun.

Alexander Daniels (5)
Ashby CE Primary School

My First Acrostic

A liens are silly.

L ook at the aliens.

I love aliens.

E very alien is different.

N o alien lives on Earth.

S even aliens came to eat.

Emma Western (5)
Ashby CE Primary School

My First Acrostic

A liens are funny.

L ots of aliens are tickly.

I love food.

E veryone has a grand time.

N o aliens don't have feet.

S ome are best.

Noah Phillips (5)
Ashby CE Primary School

Thomas

T ortoises are my favourite.

H appy and full of energy.

O wls are my favourite.

M onkeys swing.

A nts are peculiar.

S weaty socks.

Thomas Leite (6)
Brownlow CP School

Alexander

A nts are my favourite.

L oud and lively.

E xcitable.

X boxes are fun.

A lways smiling.

N early six.

D inosaurs are my favourite.

E xtra good.

R eading is my favourite.

Alexander Wood (5)
Brownlow CP School

Lottie

L ovely big girl.

O rganised all the time.

T ea is my favourite.

T eddies are my favourite.

I nteresting clothes.

E xercise is my favourite.

Lottie Evans (6)
Brownlow CP School

Leanora

L ovely big girl.

E ats lots of chocolate.

A ge 6.

N ice girl.

O range juice is my favourite.

R ainbows are my favourite.

A lways good.

Leanora Knott (6)
Brownlow CP School

Sophie

S uper, smart and sensible.

O range juice is my favourite.

P ink is my favourite colour.

H orses are my favourite animal.

I ce cream is yummy.

E veryone is my friend.

Sophie Tolton (6)
Brownlow CP School

Phillipa

P ink is my favourite colour.

H orses I like.

I ce cream is the best.

L ambs are my favourite.

L adybirds are nice.

I nsects are nice.

P addling is fun.

A pple is my favourite fruit.

Phillipa Leach (6)
Brownlow CP School

23

Daisy

elightful and kind.

lways happy and sensible.

ce cream is my favourite.

ensible and smart.

ellow is not my favourite colour.

Daisy Huddlestone (5)
Brownlow CP School

Abby

A pples are my favourite.

B each balls are my favourite.

B eautiful and kind.

Y oghurts are my favourite.

Abby Gregory (5)
Brownlow CP School

25

Matthew

M aths is my best subject.

A nimals are my favourite.

T ea I drink.

T igers I like.

H appy and good.

E xcellent boy.

W ears shorts.

Matthew Burgoine (5)
Brownlow CP School

Laura

L ovely.

A ge 6.

U nderstanding.

R aspberries are my favourite fruit.

A nimals are my favourite.

Laura Belcher (6)
Brownlow CP School

Myself

M y name is Leila

Y oung

S ensible

E ats Easter eggs

L ovely

F unny.

Leila Ladjimi (5)
Brownlow CP School

Caitlin

C hatterbox and happy.

A lways good.

I ce creams are my favourite.

T V I like to watch.

L ovely me.

I nteresting girl.

N ot naughty.

Caitlin Smallshaw (6)
Brownlow CP School

Charmice

C hatterbox and good.

H appy and beautiful.

A lways nice and kind.

R oses are my favourite flowers.

M ake-up is nice.

I njections hurt.

C asual is nice.

E xtra good and nice.

Charmice Davison (6)
Brownlow CP School

Logan

L oud and lovely.

O range juice is my favourite.

G ames I like.

A party is best.

N umbers are good.

Logan Mackie (5)
Brownlow CP School

Myself

M y name is Cameron.

Y oung.

S illy.

E ats lollipops.

L ovely.

F unny.

Cameron Pritchett (6)
Brownlow CP School

Myself

M y name is Brandon

Y oung

S ensible

E ats chocolate

L ucky

F it.

Brandon Stobart (6)
Brownlow CP School

Lara

L ovely and kind

A lways nice

R abbits I like

A nimals are my favourite.

Lara Mousley (5)
Brownlow CP School

Sophie

S ausages are the best.

O wls are my favourite bird.

P ink is my favourite.

H orses are my favourite.

I ce cream is nice.

E ating chocolate is yummy.

Sophie Norwood (5)
Brownlow CP School

Emily

E xtra kind.

M aths is the best.

I ce cream is my favourite.

L ucky girl.

Y ellow is my favourite.

Emily North (5)
Brownlow CP School

Ella

E arrings are my favourite things.

L etters are great things.

L adybirds are very nice.

A mbulances can rescue me.

Ella Steggles (6)
Brownlow CP School

Aimee

A lways nice.

I ce cream is my favourite at school.

M aths is my favourite at school.

E xtra good and sensible.

E veryone is my friend.

Aimee Majury (5)
Brownlow CP School

Monique

My name is Monique

M onique likes lollies.

O ctopus is big.

N anny cuddles me.

I like ice cream.

Q uack, quack.

U p goes the umbrella.

E lephants are big.

Monique Dobie (6)
Brownlow CP School

Jaden

My name is Jaden.

J am is my favourite.

A dog licks.

D ancing, spinning my myself.

E ggs are good.

N anny hugs me.

Jaden Gibbs (6)
Brownlow CP School

Adam

My name is Adam

A dam has some sweets

D oor rattles

A dam cuddles his nanny

M y toy is a racing car.

Adam Wallbanks (5)
Brownlow CP School

Molly

My name is Molly

M olly has blue eyes.

O ver the weekend I went to Nan's.

L ike lollies when it's hot.

L ike the sun.

Y oghurts are my favourite.

Molly Newman (6)
Brownlow CP School

Aaliyah

My name is Aaliyah.

A aliyah is happy.

A aliyah has blue eyes.

L oves lollies.

I like jelly.

Y oghurts make me healthy.

A aliyah is at school.

H orses are my favourite.

Aaliyah Johnson (6)
Brownlow CP School

Mikey

My name is Mikey

M ikey likes swimming.

I like painting.

K ites are my favourite thing.

E ggs are smelly.

Y ellow is my favourite colour.

Mikey Irish (6)
Brownlow CP School

Oliver

My name is Oliver

O range is nice.

L ike lollies.

I like football.

V ans are my favourite.

E ggs are horrible.

R ats bite hard.

Oliver Skinner (6)
Brownlow CP School

Libby

My name is Libby

L ollies are my favourite things.

I ce is my favourite thing.

B alls are my favourite thing.

B alloons are my favourite thing.

Y oghurts are my favourite thing.

Libby Duncan (6)
Brownlow CP School

Hollie

My name is Hollie

H elicopters are my favourite.

O pticians have glasses.

L orries are big.

L ollies are yummy.

I love my mummy.

E ggs are yummy.

Hollie Smith (6)
Brownlow CP School

Leah

My name is Leah

L ike princesses.

E mily is my favourite name for bunnies.

A nd for cats is kitties.

H ats, I love them because they are pink, purple and yellow.

Leah Corbett (6)
Brownlow CP School

Grace

My name is Grace

G race likes going to the park.

R aces are fun.

A pples are delicious.

C ats are beautiful.

E ggs are good.

Grace Houghton (6)
Brownlow CP School

Grace

My name is Grace

G race likes cats

R ed jumpers

A nd blue jumpers

C ats are my pets

E llis is my friend.

Grace Weston (5)
Brownlow CP School

Charlotte

My name is Charlotte

C harlotte likes dogs

H orses are my favourite thing

A pples are yummy

R ebecca is cute

L oves lollies

O liver is my best friend

T eecky is cuddly

T eecky is my teddy

E vie is my second best friend.

Charlotte Smith (6)
Brownlow CP School

George

My name is George

Giraffes are one of my favourites

Elephants are big but I am small

Oliver is my friend

Running makes me fit

Gorillas are black and hairy like my grandad

Ellis in Year 6 is my friend.

George Lawrance (6)
Brownlow CP School

Jodie

My name is Jodie

J odie likes jelly
O ff go the lights on our day
D o you like jam on your toast?
I like jam on my toast, yes
E vie is my friend.

Jodie Plowman (6)
Brownlow CP School

Connie

My name is Connie.

C onnie likes football.

O ranges are good.

N ew motorbikes.

N ew motorbikes.

I like skateboarding.

E ggs are healthy.

Connie Harrison (6)
Brownlow CP School

Harry

H appy and helpful.

A pples I like.

R ockets and robots I like.

R eading I like.

Y oghurts I like.

Harry Digby (6)
Brownlow CP School

Lions

L ion is angry

I t eats meat

O range fur

N ice brown eyes

S leepy yawns.

Reece Brown (7)
Knighton Fields Primary School

My First Acrostic - Leicestershire

Owl

O range eyes.

W hite feathers.

L ikes to eat mice.

Fen Sealey (7)
Knighton Fields Primary School

Lions

L ions have black stripes.

I t has 4 legs.

O ne long tail.

N eeds meat to keep them going.

S leeps in a jungle.

Jack Youmans (7)
Knighton Fields Primary School

Monkeys

M onkeys fool about like me.

O ver trees and swings.

N ice funny faces.

K eeping me entertained.

E very child laughs at them.

Y ou always want to take them home.

Aston Clarke (7)
Knighton Fields Primary School

Tiger Facts

T eeth are really big.

I ndia and China.

G rowls very, very loud.

E ats zebras.

R uns very fast.

Hollie Pugh (7)
Knighton Fields Primary School

Monkey

M onkeys mess about in trees.

O n branches swinging about.

N ight-time monkeys are asleep.

K rzysztof likes monkeys.

E ats yellow bananas.

Y ells *aarrrar!*

Kyle Connelly-Coles (7)
Knighton Fields Primary School

61

Monkeys

onkeys hang from trees.

ther monkeys live with each other.

ight-time monkeys sleep with each other.

rzysztof likes monkeys.

ggs are Italian monkey's favourite food.

awning brown monkeys.

Chay Parker (6)
Knighton Fields Primary School

Rabbit

R un rabbits run

A lways eat grass

B eautiful rabbit

B urrowing holes

I nto the ground

T eeth that stick out.

Chloe Staniforth (7)
Knighton Fields Primary School

Lion

L ions run 70 miles an hour!

I n Africa

O range skin

N oisy lions roar!

Marvin Etukudoh (6)
Knighton Fields Primary School

Sea Horse

S hy as a mouse

E ats seaweed.

A n endangered creature.

H orse-like creature.

O r you could call it the horse of the sea.

R ound it goes, like a racing car.

S ea horses can change colour.

E verywhere.

Luke Fradsham (7)
New Swannington Primary School

Clownfish

C amouflage like a tiger.

L ow down in the water.

O range and

W hite stripes.

N ever alone.

F ish are friends.

I t is sting-proof.

S wimming around

H appy as can be.

Matthew Johnson (7)
New Swannington Primary School

Sea Horse

S wirly

E legant

A mazing

H appy

O ut of this world

R ound tail

S wimming fast

E xtraordinary.

Rosie Kelly (6)
New Swannington Primary School

Shark

S piky and sharp.

H ungry for fish

A nd big jaws.

R eady to eat his food.

K ind of greedy.

Libby Heathcote (6)
New Swannington Primary School

Crab

C rawls along the sand

R azor-sharp claws

A nd it scrabbles along

B ut it's always about.

Leah Jeffs (7)
New Swannington Primary School

Crab

C rabs snap.

R ip.

A hard shell.

B est king.

Callum McIlvenna (6)
New Swannington Primary School

Shark

S wim in the sea

H ungry

A nd wide jaw

R eady to pounce

K ing of the sea.

Chloe Winter (6)
New Swannington Primary School

Shark

S harp teeth.

H e's hungry a lot.

A nd he has big teeth.

R eally huge in the sea.

K ing of the sea.

Ria Kaur (6)
New Swannington Primary School

Baby Dolphins

B aby dolphins wait to be born.

A nd snuggle in mummy's tummy.

B aby dolphins are cute.

'Y ay,' said the baby.

D olphins diving back in.

O h I hope they have fun.

L ittle dolphins play in the pool.

P lenty of room to play.

H eavy daddy dolphin splashes.

I said to Mummy, 'It's too heavy!'

'N o, it's fun,' said Mummy.

Lauren Grice (6)
New Swannington Primary School

Shark

S harks have sharp teeth

H e eats fish

A nd swims fast

R eady to gobble up fish

K ing of all the fish.

Ben Rhodes (7)
New Swannington Primary School

Easter Eggs

E ggs

A nd chocolate

S ome Easter eggs

T ry to get an Easter egg

E veryone happy

R abbits.

E at an Easter egg

G et an Easter egg

G et an Easter egg for everyone.

S ee, it's Easter.

Joshua Pearson (5)
New Swannington Primary School

Shark

S harp teeth

H eavy

A ngry

R umbling tummy

K illing shark.

Oliver Moseley (5)
New Swannington Primary School

Chick

C racking through the shell.

H atching out.

I n a nest, high in the trees.

C rack out the shell.

K eep safe.

Morgan Butcher (5)
New Swannington Primary School

Shark

S wimming in the sea.

H aving something to eat.

A nice time.

R ipping up fish.

K illing squids.

Ellie Stokes (6)
New Swannington Primary School

Shark

S harp teeth.

H ungry mouth.

A wavy tail.

R umbly belly.

K iller.

Jake Barry (5)
New Swannington Primary School

Spring

S unny.

P retty flowers growing.

R eaching for the sun.

I like spring.

N ights get shorter.

G reen grass.

Molly Hall (6)
New Swannington Primary School

Shark

S wimming slowly through the sea

H ungry to catch their prey

A ngry-looking eyes

R eally fierce teeth

K eep away.

Alyssa Harris (6)
New Swannington Primary School

Bunny

B unny hop

U nder a tree

N aughty bunny

N ibbling

Y our knee.

Joseph Wardle (5)
New Swannington Primary School

My First Acrostic - Leicestershire

Easter

E aster bunnies

A n Easter egg

S pring

T eddy bear

E aster baskets

R un at Easter.

Arian Cornforth-Steen (5)
New Swannington Primary School

Starfish

S harp spines.

T rickling in the rock pool.

I nteresting arms.

R ed, orange and yellow.

F ind me if you can.

I n the deep sea.

S pots on my body.

H appy.

Neve Clarke (5)
New Swannington Primary School

Chick

C ute little chicks

H ug each other

I n the nest

C uddly, yellow fluff

K ind and happy.

Ben Crutchley (6)
New Swannington Primary School

Puffer Fish

F unny fins

I n the sea

S illy body

H uff, puff, pufferfish.

Lewis Kent (5)
New Swannington Primary School

Fish

F unny big eyes.

I n the deep blue sea.

S wimming with a swishing tail.

H appy as can be.

Joseph Smedley (5)
New Swannington Primary School

Fish

F an tail fish

I n the sea

S wimming

H appy fish.

Elliot Jackson (5)
New Swannington Primary School

Easter Rabbit

R abbits are fluffy

A nd they like carrots

B ut they like cabbage

B ouncy, bouncy bunny

I have a rabbit

T he rabbit has long ears.

Thomas Horn (6)
New Swannington Primary School

Butterfly

B eautiful

U p

T insel

T inky

E aty

R inky

F iffy

L ike

Y ellow.

Jack Stretton (5)
New Swannington Primary School

Frogs

F rogs
R ush
O n
G reen
S lime.

Aaron Butler (4)
New Swannington Primary School

Frogs

F rogs

R ush

O ver

G reen

S lime.

Findlay Mitchell (5)
New Swannington Primary School

Frog

F rog

R ibbits

O n

G rass.

Kloe Fessey-Clifton (5)
New Swannington Primary School

Tadpole

T iny

A nimal

D ot

P addling

O n

L ily pad

E ating.

Abigail Twigg (5)
New Swannington Primary School

Butterfly

B eautiful

U p

T ree

T op

E gg

R ed

F ly

L et

Y ellow.

Harvey Burbank (5)
New Swannington Primary School

Tadpole

T iny

A nimal

D ot

P ole

O ff

L ow

E gg.

Oliver Springthorpe (5)
New Swannington Primary School

Fish

F ish go to sea to eat

I n the sea fish are happy

S ea is see-through

H appy fish hunt for food.

Harrison Ison (7)
New Swannington Primary School

Eggs, Eggs

E aster time

G iving eggs away

G ive up eating chocolate

S un at Easter time.

Benjamin Knight (5)
New Swannington Primary School

Emily

E very day I go to see my friend at school.

M y favourite animal is a Labrador dog.

I like pink candyfloss because it is lovely.

L ove swimming pools and playing football.

Y o-yos are my favourite toy.

Emily Stone (6)
Orchard CE Primary School

Sophie

S ophie is my name and I am very special,

O ranges are my second favourite fruit,

P oetry is my favourite sort of writing to read aloud,

H onesty is very important to me and my family,

I 'm very intelligent,

E ntering competitions I really enjoy.

Sophie Perrett (7)
Orchard CE Primary School

Giada

G oing on holiday is my favourite thing,

I love High School Musical,

A nd I like singing and dancing,

D oing gymnastics is my favourite thing to do,

A pples are my favourite fruit.

Giada Manuele (7)
Orchard CE Primary School

Beth

B utterflies are my favourite insect,

E very time I go to the cinema I eat sweets,

T uesday is swimming day,

H orses are my favourite animals.

Beth Quittenton (6)
Orchard CE Primary School

My First Acrostic - Leicestershire

Lucy

L icking lollies is fun,

U mbrellas are colourful, my favourite colour is yellow,

C hocolate is very yummy to eat,

Y ellow is my favourite colour in the rainbow.

Lucy McDonald (7)
Orchard CE Primary School

Isabelle

I 'm intelligent,

S wimming is one of my hobbies,

A pples are my favourite fruit,

B aths are my favourite,

E nthusiastic was what I was made for,

L earning is one of my hobbies,

L ovely is what I always am,

E ggs are my favourite food.

Isabelle O'Connell (7)
Orchard CE Primary School

Katie

K atie really likes swimming,

A lways enjoys horse riding,

T ea is my favourite drink,

I like dancing,

E ntering competitions is something I like to do.

Katie Gudgeon (7)
Orchard CE Primary School

Eva

E njoys swimming and playing kindly,

V ery helpful and caring to friends,

A lways happy and sharing.

Eva Blockley-Orton (7)
Orchard CE Primary School

My First Acrostic - Leicestershire

Mia

M ia likes dancing lots,

I like art and making things,

A nts don't like me very much.

Mia Brindley (7)
Orchard CE Primary School

Rachel

R eading, relaxing, enjoying my time,

A lways likes going to the fair,

C hilling out on the sofa watching TV,

H ave a hamster called Henry, he is very lazy,

E xtremely excited all the time,

L icking lollies is very tasty.

Rachel Bowkett (7)
Orchard CE Primary School

Emily

E very day I like to play in the garden,

M onday is special at school because it is PE,

I like fish and chips because they are yummy,

L oves going to school,

Y oghurt is nice for pudding, it's healthy.

Emily Blyth (6)
Orchard CE Primary School

Chloe

C heerful and kind is what I am,

H elpful to my mummy,

L ooking after my little brother makes me happy,

O ranges are my favourite fruit,

E njoy laughing every day.

Chloe Barry (7)
Orchard CE Primary School

Izzy

I have a rabbit called Crystal, I like to play with her,

Z ebras are my second favourite animals,

Z oos hold animals which I like,

Y ellow is one of my favourite colours.

Izzy Cantillon (7)
Orchard CE Primary School

The Lizard

L izards sneaking across the rock,

I n the old rocks they sneak,

Z ebras stomp on them,

A lizard is sneaky,

R oams,

D igs all day and all night,

S aid they run fast.

Felix George Roome (6)
St Bartholomew's CE Primary School, Loughborough

Bats

B abies are tiny,

A nxious not to be seen,

T ugs up tight, upside down.

Emily Reed (7)
St Bartholomew's CE Primary School, Loughborough

Panda

P andas eat bamboo,

A panda is like a teddy bear,

N ights, the panda goes to sleep,

D eep in the forest the pandas fight,

A nd their fur is black and white.

Olivia Johnstone (7)
St Bartholomew's CE Primary School, Loughborough

Shark

S cary enormous shark,

H eaving through the deep dark sea,

A sking for his food,

R ound the whole of the sea it goes,

K ind is not for a shark!

Caitlin Errington (7)
St Bartholomew's CE Primary School, Loughborough

Sparrow

S ings beautifully,

P icking on the tree,

A bird is always nice,

R oaming about,

R ustling in the trees,

O range feathers,

W atching the children down below.

Mollie Smith (7)
St Bartholomew's CE Primary School, Loughborough

Starfish

S ome starfish hide in the seaweed,

T iny shells surround it,

A long the sand it goes,

R apidly waving its points around,

F ast, it's floating around

I n the sea,

S ee them glide,

H e/she hides all the time.

Kit Jackson (7)
St Bartholomew's CE Primary School, Loughborough

Sharky Sharky!

§ uspicious because of a fish,

Ħ unger through its body,

Å sking for food,

Ŗ acing around,

Ķ illing fish.

Alexandra Here (6)
St Bartholomew's CE Primary School, Loughborough

Hummingbird

H appy chirping all the time,

U nder leaves it sweeps all night,

M aking happy noises all the day long,

M ore or less beautiful it gets each day,

I n the sky they like to fly,

N ight and day they chirp happily,

G racefully they flap around, high up in the sky,

B eing kind and gentle to its family,

I n the sky it likes to fly,

R ound and round it likes to play,

D ancing in the sky very happily.

Katherine Louise Stevens (6)
St Bartholomew's CE Primary School, Loughborough

Penguin

P enguins laying eggs,

E ating fish all day long,

N ight is their favourite time,

G oing to dive in the sea,

U nder the deep blue sea,

I ce is fun when you're me,

N ice penguins, 1, 2, 3, in water, *wheeee!*

Jade Weston (7)
St Bartholomew's CE Primary School, Loughborough

Rabbit

R unning quickly across the grass,

A lways eating carrots,

B ad fox chasing him,

B irds flying overhead,

I nside his hole now,

T ail curled up.

Lydia Gray (7)
St Bartholomew's CE Primary School, Loughborough

Parrot

P erching on a back branch,

A nd squawking,

R unning across the grass,

R oaming in the sky,

O n top of the tree,

T alking weirdly.

Ella Douglas (7)
St Bartholomew's CE Primary School, Loughborough

Dolphin

D oing tricks,

O pening her mouth and catching fish,

L apping side to side,

P inching fish,

H iding from hunters,

I n the water all the time except meal times,

N ibbling some fish in the ocean!

Ellie Hooper (7)
St Bartholomew's CE Primary School, Loughborough

Wolf

Wide open jaws,
On top of his prey,
Long, long tail,
Fast running.

Elliot Kelly (6)
St Bartholomew's CE Primary School, Loughborough

Alligator

A mean animal hunting for food,

L ong tail lying down on long green grass,

L ies there for a very long while,

I n it goes in the river,

G oes along happily swimming,

A quiet animal when it sleeps,

T errifying animal,

O pens its mouth widely to eat,

R ips its prey's skin.

Beth Willett (6)
St Bartholomew's CE Primary School, Loughborough

Sparrow

S wooping sparrow darting in the clouds, wings as fluffy as wool,

P erching in its nice new nest as soft as fur,

A crobatic in the air,

R eaching the sky,

R ummaging through leaves leaving its nest,

O ver the hills and far away lives the sparrow,

W arming its babies, keeping them close.

Eve Willett (6)
St Bartholomew's CE Primary School, Loughborough

My First Acrostic - Leicestershire

Goldfish

G ood little goldfish pushing himself through the water,
Looking out for danger,

O range, old, ordinary goldfish swimming through the water,

L oud footsteps bumping the ground immediately waiting
For the goldfish,

D anger is coming for the goldfish, it quickly finds a hiding place,

F ox is waiting outside of the water,
It licks its lips while waiting still,

I llness comes inside the goldfish,

S till waiting for the goldfish,

H ard rocks, the goldfish feels, the fox dips his head in the pond,
It snaps its teeth together and eats the goldfish and runs home.

Jaya Patel (6)
St Bartholomew's CE Primary School, Loughborough

Hippopotamus

H ungry jumping hippo

I tching its skin

P lated thick skins

P apered platted skin

O pened its massive jaws

P ainful when its hurts itself

O ver the plants his massive jaws bite

T iptoeing is rubbish,

A rching his scary jaws

M unching hungry hippo

U nder rocks he can't hide

S ometimes he gets in mud.

Imogen & Josh McDougall (7)
St Bartholomew's CE Primary School, Loughborough

Eagles

E agles have eyes as dark as coal,

A n eagle can dive down like an arrow,

G rasp the prey's belly,

L unging at little fish in the sea,

E agles tear fishes' guts apart.

Alec William Gregory (7)
St Bartholomew's CE Primary School, Loughborough

Tortoise

T iny tortoise talking to his friend,

O n top of the grass he sits,

R ock hard shell to keep it safe,

T ired tortoise in the winter,

O r in the summer he stays awake,

I n his hut, he stays most of the day,

S lowly plodding along,

E ars hiding in its shells.

Kezia Arina Rodgers (7)
St Bartholomew's CE Primary School, Loughborough

Badger

B ig badger in the garden,

A wake all night and sleeping all day,

D anger ahead down in the bush,

G arden is where I eat,

E legant paws and claws are sharp,

R un, run, jump in the hole quickly,

In the muddy water for a bath.

Tess Lucie Duffin (6)
St Bartholomew's CE Primary School, Loughborough

Peacock

P roudly walking peacock,

E ating peacock pecking at corn,

A lways showing off,

C laws as sharp as knives,

O n the ground, never in the air,

C onfident in every way,

K eeps all its nice feathers.

Miah Proud (6)
St Bartholomew's CE Primary School, Loughborough

Donkey

D ragging his big back,

O n the grass he is sleeping,

N o danger,

K nowing when people are there,

E ating the grass with his jaws,

Y awning at the sandy beach,

   Smelling the food when people are eating.

Jacob Bott (7)
St Bartholomew's CE Primary School, Loughborough

Starfish

S lippery starfish swimming in the sea,

T hen he fell down on the ground,

A nd he was shiny,

R umbling sea wiped the starfish out,

F inding his way back home,

I mmediately a shark came round,

S *nap* went the shark,

H e missed the starfish.

Max Cunliffe (6)
St Bartholomew's CE Primary School, Loughborough

Giraffe

G reat long neck reaching up high,

I t has long legs,

R eaching up high and eating leaves,

A s tall as a tree,

F inding patches of grass,

F inding trees to eat off,

E ating all the leaves.

Harry Maltby (7)
St Bartholomew's CE Primary School, Loughborough

Elephant

🄴 lephant lies in the sun,

🄻 azily waking up in the beautiful sun,

🄴 lephant edges towards the river,

🄿 eter her son, is as grey as a stone,

🄷 enry her other son is too,

🄰 merican elephants lumber to land,

🄽 aughty elephant squirts out water,

🅃 owards the end of the day, the elephants go to sleep.

Isobel Henderson (6)
St Bartholomew's CE Primary School, Loughborough

Kangaroo

K angaroo as jumpy as a Jack-in-the-box,

A fterwards she gets a bit tired,

N ever stopping all that jumping,

G oing along quickly,

A mazingly strong hopping along,

R unning round all day,

O off out into the desert,

O h, she never stops.

Laura Henderson (6)
St Bartholomew's CE Primary School, Loughborough

Pheasant

P heasants are the birds that can't fly very well,

H eads that are very green,

E ats a lot of seeds,

A t good times,

S o good, getting better at a lot of things,

A lways beautiful at all times,

N ot fit at all because they can't run fast,

T alking to their best friends.

Ben Ragg (7)
St Bartholomew's CE Primary School, Loughborough

Squirrel

S neaky squirrel stealing nuts,

Q ueen of the squirrels quarrelling,

U nderstanding trees,

I nterested fox creeping along,

R eaching and climbing, never giving up,

R ound eyes focused on his nut,

E ach nut as tasty as chocolate,

L eaping around.

Kieran (6)
St Bartholomew's CE Primary School, Loughborough

Butterfly

B eautiful butterfly black and orange,

U mbrellas covered the sky for the butterflies,

T he butterflies' wings are so shiny,

T ight wings and silk colours,

E very butterfly is elegant,

R aising through the air,

F luttering their wings,

L ying like a butterfly,

Y ou can fly like a butterfly.

Izzy Rose Misir (7)
St Bartholomew's CE Primary School, Loughborough

Hedgehog

H iding from the cold,

E very time it sleeps, it is warm as your teddy in your bed,

D reaming of wonderful things,

G o and wake up because it's summertime,

E very day hunting for slugs and snails,

H unting and hunting but can't find any food,

O pen your eyes sleepyhead,

G o out of your garden, it's summer.

Isabel Adlam (7)
St Bartholomew's CE Primary School, Loughborough

Spider

S pooky spider making a web,

P icking up a fly behind me,

I n its web, it is going to eat the fly,

D oes the spider like drinking blood at lunchtime?

E ye as sharp as a shark,

R ound eyes and black skin and long 8 legs.

Anika Gohel (7)
St Bartholomew's CE Primary School, Loughborough

My First Acrostic - Leicestershire

Ostrich

O strich as furry as a fluffy ball,

S earching with their smell to search for nuts,

T alks a lot, moves fast and slow in the blazing sun,

R ound, rich ostrich,

I n a glinting desert,

C lean as a shiny stone,

H eavy ostrich you can never fly.

Eleanor Hall (7)
St Bartholomew's CE Primary School, Loughborough

Dolphin

ipping dolphin swimming in the water,

pening his mouth and squeaking,

eaps high in the air and eats fish,

eople feed them by throwing the food,

appy dolphins are smiling,

nteresting dolphins flipping in the air,

odding dolphins are cute.

Sam Keane (6)
St Bartholomew's CE Primary School, Loughborough

Spring

S un is shining up in the sky,

P arents are going on holiday in spring,

R ain is good for the plants,

I n spring the parents are resting,

N ice weather in spring,

G reen grass growing.

Kamran Samra (6)
Sandfield Close Primary School

Spring

S un is the best,

P retty purple flowers are growing,

R ain is good for the plants,

I n spring plants are growing,

N ice grass is growing,

G reat time to play out.

Rianna Rajani (6)
Sandfield Close Primary School

Spring

S pring is beautiful,

P lants are growing,

R ain is fun,

I n spring there are nice things,

N ice day,

G reen grass is growing.

Mohammed Idris Adam (5)
Sandfield Close Primary School

Spring

S pring,

P urple flowers,

R oses,

I like playing outside,

N ice spring,

G rass is growing.

Kabir Singh Kalsi (5)
Sandfield Close Primary School

Indiah

I really enjoy typing on the computer,

N umeracy is quite fun, mostly these days,

D ecember I love the most,

I ndya is my friend forever,

A ll my friends admire me but I admire them,

H arleen is my other friend forever.

Indiah Parmar (7)
Sandfield Close Primary School

Vaishali

V aishali, that's me,

A little breeze on my knees,

I ndoor play,

S unshine bay,

H i, Vaishali at your service,

A s pretty as can be,

L oves me, tee-hee,

I care, I care, but . . . I feel like a pear.

Vaishali Asawala (7)
Sandfield Close Primary School

AKshay

A kshay is here,

K unal is my best friend,

S ome delicious activities, yippee,

H ey I am good at football,

A t school I do activities,

Y ippee, I am at school.

Akshay Pancholi (6)
Sandfield Close Primary School

Parth

P ractise my times table,

A lways works hard and concentrates,

R unning to see what's going on,

T aking my time on my work,

H iding and playing outside is fun.

Parth Shah (6)
Sandfield Close Primary School

Zishaan

Z ishaan is here,

I 'm a good boy,

S ometimes I make friends,

H ey, good work Zishaan,

A m a quiet boy,

A m a good worker,

N ice work.

Zishaan Sumra (6)
Sandfield Close Primary School

Hari

H earing the breeze floating in the sky,

A nger just goes flying by,

R amayan I like to see,

I n my house I watch TV.

Hemish Khera (7)
Sandfield Close Primary School

Vinaya

V inny they call me,

I maginary things I see,

N ice and clever,

A gain I see,

Y ay, party time,

A way I go.

Vinaya Patel (7)
Sandfield Close Primary School

Mansi

M arvellous me, ready to be,

A mazing artwork to be seen,

N ervous me, I'm so fun,

S uper me, I'm a number one chum,

I nnocent me, I'm so yum, yum.

Mansi Patel (6)
Sandfield Close Primary School

Shanil

S hani plays football,

H ot on the grass,

A nd I feel fat,

N il-nil in a football match,

I see a bee all around me,

L et me see how you make tea.

Shanil Sodha (7)
Sandfield Close Primary School

Karan

K aran is my name,

A mazing things happen to me,

R eady to play always,

A ll my friends are nice to me,

N o one thinks that I am short.

Karan Mehta (7)
Sandfield Close Primary School

Preesha

P ink is my favourite colour,

R E is OK to me,

E ager me, ready to learn about badgers,

E xcellent runner,

S ome scrumptious, delicious chocolate cake,

H ome time, yippee,

A ll my friends admire me.

Preesha Lad (6)
Sandfield Close Primary School

Kieran

K ieran is my name,

I am a grand footballer,

E xcellent footballer,

R unning all around,

A m I tall?

N ot at all.

Kieran Taank (7)
Sandfield Close Primary School

Indya

I am going to tell you about my life,

N umeracy is OK to me,

D ecember is my favourite month,

Y um, I really like auntie Margaret's chocolate sponge,

A mazing friends I have and they are called Indiah and Harleen.

Indya Madlani (7)
Sandfield Close Primary School

Alim

A t a football match, I

L ike to kick the ball,

I like to play football and I like to score,

M atches are my best thing.

Alim Somani (6)
Sandfield Close Primary School

Prem

P laying pizza games,

R unning to see what's going on,

E very day I learn,

M aking new friends.

Prem Daudia (7)
Sandfield Close Primary School

Rohan

R ohan is an intelligent brother,

O h I'm fantastic,

H andwriting I love to show off,

A lot of friends I have,

N obody wants to leave me.

Rohan Joshi (6)
Sandfield Close Primary School

Roshni

R eady to go,

O nly the best at numeracy,

S uper me, I'm a number one star,

H ere is a parcel for me,

N umeracy and literacy is the best,

I ncredible me!

Roshni Parekh (6)
Sandfield Close Primary School

Spring

Ⓢ pring is fun because the sun will shine,

Ⓟ retty little purple flowers,

Ⓡ ain is good for the plants,

Ⓘ n spring the plants need water,

Ⓝ ice grass is growing,

Ⓖ reen grass is growing and shiny.

Punam Patel (5)
Sandfield Close Primary School

Spring

S un is shining high and high up in the sky,

P retty flowers are growing in the green grass,

R ed birds are flying around the sky,

I like spring because lots of beautiful flowers are growing,

N ice and lovely leaves,

G reen grass is growing very long.

Krish Nigam (5)
Sandfield Close Primary School

Spring

S pring is warm,

P ink flowers,

R ed flowers,

I 'm happy,

N ice day,

G reen plants.

Payal Shavji (5)
Sandfield Close Primary School

Spring

S pring helps the flowers,

P lants are starting to grow in the spring,

R ain is good for the plants,

I like the rain, the rain is lovely,

N ice grass is growing,

G reen grass is shining bright because the sun is out.

Shreena Daudia (6)
Sandfield Close Primary School

169

Spring

S un is shining high in the sky,

P elicans out standing,

R eally long grass,

I like spring because lots of beautiful flowers grow,

N ice grass and trees are lovely,

G rass is long and tall.

Maitri Brahmbhatt (5)
Sandfield Close Primary School

Spring

S pring is pretty,

P retty flowers in spring,

R ains sometimes,

I n spring it is cold,

N ow it is nice,

G reen grass.

Mario Modha (5)
Sandfield Close Primary School

Spring

S pring is a lovely season because flowers start to grow,

P retty purple flowers,

R eally long grass,

I love the sunshine,

N ice fantastic weather,

G reat busy bumblebees flying everywhere.

Shreya Kotecha (5)
Sandfield Close Primary School

Spring

S un comes out in spring,

P erfect days in springtime,

R ain makes the flowers grow,

I nside people keep flowers in their houses,

N ow the plants are growing,

G reen grass grows in spring.

Himani Mistry (6)
Sandfield Close Primary School

Spring

S hiny, shiny sun comes out in spring, to make the world warm,

P erfect days in spring make it perfect to play outside,

R ain and sun make flowers grow in spring,

I n spring baby animals are born,

N ow new grass is growing in spring,

G irls and boys love spring.

Alisha Sedani (5)
Sandfield Close Primary School

Spring

S un comes out in spring,

P erfect days in spring,

R ain makes flowers grow in spring,

I nsects fly in the air in spring,

N ew flowers start to grow,

G reen grass grows in spring.

Rishit Bhatt (6)
Sandfield Close Primary School

Spring

S un comes out in spring,

P retty flowers grow in spring,

R abbits come out at night,

I n spring flowers grow,

N ew flowers grow in spring,

G rass grows in spring.

Annil Gamsi (5)
Sandfield Close Primary School

Spring

S un comes out in spring,

P lants grow in the pots,

R ain makes plants grow in spring,

I love spring because I can play outside,

N ice long days in spring,

G row flowers, grow.

Muntazir Haji (6)
Sandfield Close Primary School

Spring

S un comes out in spring,

P erfect days in spring,

R ain makes flowers grow,

I n spring chicks and lambs begin to hatch,

N ow the flowers begin to grow in spring,

G rass grows in spring.

Veer Kukadia (6)
Sandfield Close Primary School

Spring

S un comes out in spring,

P erfect days in spring,

R ain comes quite a lot,

I like spring,

N ice days in spring,

G reen shiny green grass.

Kavil Sanghera (5)
Sandfield Close Primary School

Spring

S pring is nice and I like to play in spring,

P lants grow in spring,

R abbits jump out in spring,

I like to play in spring,

N ow the flowers start to grow,

G reen grass grows in spring.

Jasneet Sangha (5)
Sandfield Close Primary School

Spring

S un comes out in spring

P erfect days in spring

R abbits hop around

I n spring the flowers start to grow

N ice days in spring

G reen grass grows in spring.

Jade Shergold (5)
Sandfield Close Primary School

Spring

S un comes out in spring,

P erfect days in spring,

R ain comes quite a lot,

I like spring,

N ice days in spring,

G reen shiny green grass.

Nayan Khan (5)
Sandfield Close Primary School

Spring

S pring is a lovely season,

P lants grow in spring,

R ain makes plants grow,

I like to play outside in spring,

N ew lambs are born,

G reen grass grows in spring.

Ajay Vegad (6)
Sandfield Close Primary School

Spring

S un comes out in spring,

P lants start to grow in spring,

R ain makes plants grow,

I n spring plants grow in spring,

N ice season in spring,

G ood days in spring.

Sunny Rana (5)
Sandfield Close Primary School

Spring

S pring is a nice lovely season,

P retty flowers start to grow,

R abbits come out in spring,

I like spring because I get to play outside,

N ice flowers growing,

G reen grass grows.

Kanaya Karia (5)
Sandfield Close Primary School

Spring

S un comes out in spring,

P erfect days in spring,

R ain falls in spring to help flowers grow,

I n spring baby lambs start to grow,

N ew flowers grow in spring,

G o and play in spring.

Om Rajpara (6)
Sandfield Close Primary School

Spring

S pring is fun,

P op up flowers,

R ain helps flowers grow,

I love spring,

N ever pick flowers,

G reat spring, loves spring.

Tia Kumar (6)
Sandfield Close Primary School

Spring

S un makes flowers grow,

P erfect days for flowers to grow,

R ain makes flowers grow bigger,

I n spring plants start growing colourful flowers,

N ice days for picnics,

G reen leaves everywhere.

Shradha Rayarel (6)
Sandfield Close Primary School

Spring

S unflowers come out in spring,

P lay outside,

R ain and water helps,

I know about spring,

N ow you can enjoy spring,

G rass grows in spring.

Niken Valambhia (6)
Sandfield Close Primary School

Spring

S pring is coming now and the flowers are starting to grow,

P urple flowers are growing up in the grass,

R ain is good for the flowers,

I n the garden,

N ice lovely spring,

G reen grass is nice.

Deep Valambhia
Sandfield Close Primary School

Spring

S un is shining around us and others,

P lants are growing,

R ain is falling sometimes,

I like the leaves,

N ice colourful leaves are falling down,

G reen grass is growing very long.

Kailan Samir Gandhi (6)
Sandfield Close Primary School

Spring

S pring grows all of the plants,

P lants take the water in through leaves,

R oots keep the plants in place,

I n sunny days it's nice,

N ice weather, children play,

G reen grass.

Aryan Patel (6)
Sandfield Close Primary School

Treasure Chest

T here was a terrible fight and the treasure chest fell out to sea,

R usty, dusty treasure chest with lots of old things from ages ago,

E aster eggs in the dull, brown, black treasure chest,

A black and white pirate hat and an eagle picked me
up and dropped me,

S hiny silver sword, gold and bronze laying flat in the chest,

U nderground buried deep, it was muddy,

R ug-like mat laid on the chest,

E xciting things buried inside, shiny and glittery.

Manan Patel (6)
Sandfield Close Primary School

Treasure Chest

T reasure don't go away,

R ing is in your treasure box,

E aster eggs are inside your box,

A nd then come back to school,

S mall shiny stuff I want,

U uum, you look excited,

R ight you look beautiful,

E very day I will look at you.

Rahul Joshi (6)
Sandfield Close Primary School

Treasure Chest

T reasure chest from 200 years ago,

R usty, dusty treasure chest in the sand,

E normous treasure chest,

A mazing rings and fantastic, beautiful necklaces and diamonds,

S tinky, pinky treasure,

U pset, I am very upset because my owner is not here,

R ings are beautiful,

E uro coins in the box.

Joshan Singh (7)
Sandfield Close Primary School

Treasure Chest

This treasure chest is old and dusty,

Really alive in real life,

Eagles found the old, dusty and rusty chest,

Amazing Easter eggs inside it,

Sand on the island, that's where I fell,

Under the sun, it sat for ages,

Round there were hundreds of elephants,

Elephants were making lots of noise.

Ria Chandarana (7)
Sandfield Close Primary School

Treasure Chest

T errifying beautiful treasure chest that has a game,

R escue the treasure chest, it is in the sea,

E normous treasure chest that has lots of food,

A lphabetical sounds that can speak,

S ilky sand around me,

U gly dragon that can fly,

R ed pirate's hat is really big,

E agles that can get the treasure chest.

Prabjot Mattu (7)
Sandfield Close Primary School

Treasure Chest

T reasure chest from 8,000 years ago,

R usty treasure in the sea,

E normous shark,

A mazing jewels and fantastic necklaces,

S tiff statues,

U pset I am because my friend is not here,

R ings, diamonds,

E uro coins in the box.

Ram Pankhania (7)
Sandfield Close Primary School

Treasure Chest

T reasure don't go forever,

R ight in the sand there is treasure,

E aster egg is in the box,

A nd the treasure goes to school,

S mall diamonds were safe,

U nhappy it was,

R ed gold from the treasure chest,

E aster egg.

Divyen Popat (6)
Sandfield Close Primary School

Treasure Chest

T reasure, treasure, old dusty treasure,

R usty, rusty and sandy chest outside,

E aster eggs inside the treasure chest,

A tlantic ocean, floating nearby,

S hiny big treasure chest,

U s to you, I wonder what's in you?

R usty, rusty black treasure chest,

E xcited, excited what's inside it?

Dheesha Parmar (7)
Sandfield Close Primary School

Treasure Chest

T he pirates had a massive fight,

R eally strange for me and the pirates,

E aster eggs in my enormous treasure chest,

A n eagle picked me up and dropped me,

S uspicious shiny gold in the chest,

U nder the ground I was buried in the sand,

R usty sand I had to eat,

E xcitedly things buried inside.

Arjun Dattani (7)
Sandfield Close Primary School

Treasure Chest

The treasure chest was found in deep, deep, dark sand,

Really heavy hats and sparkly jewels,

Everything was nice before I landed on a dirty island,

A really enormous, huge, gigantic pirate bumped into me,

Something twisty and turning in here,

Under the sand is where I was buried,

Really old-fashioned toys might be in me,

Everything around me is alive.

Sophiya Sian (6)
Sandfield Close Primary School

Treasure Chest

T his treasure was found in the deep blue sea,

R eal pirates were there and they dropped me,

E verything I saw was alive,

A magical costume came on me in the sea,

S ome diamonds and pearls came in the dark blue sea,

U nderwater there were so many bubbles,

R eally old costumes to wear,

E lephants came to say bye.

Ria Pattani (7)
Sandfield Close Primary School

Treasure Chest

Treasure chest on the river, you sail away really far,
Rusty treasure chest you come to us from nasty
people from far away,
Enormous treasure chest, you are really heavy,
Amazing things might come to you like fairy dust,
Smelly socks and smelly gold treasure, a lot of
smelly things will come,
Unhappy the pirates will be without the treasure,
Really, really nice things will come in the treasure chest,
Even there might be chocolate coins!

Nikita Parmar (7)
Sandfield Close Primary School

Treasure Chest

T reasure from a nasty war with sharp swords,

R usty, rusty treasure box, where's the dusty treasure box?

E aster eggs, chocolate eggs hiding away,

A ll pirates sailing on the big waves on the sea,

S andy, sandy covering the treasure box,

U nder the deep sea swimming to the island,

R usty, rusty, old dusty, where is the key?

E aster eggs in there but how many buttons?

Tai Prasher-Lin (6)
Sandfield Close Primary School

Young Writers Information

We hope you have enjoyed reading this book - and that you will continue to enjoy it in the coming years.

If you like reading and writing poetry drop us a line, or give us a call, and we'll send you a free information pack.

Alternatively if you would like to order further copies of this book or any of our other titles, then please give us a call or log onto our website at www.youngwriters.co.uk.

Young Writers Information
Remus House ·
Coltsfoot Drive
Peterborough
PE2 9JX
(01733) 890066